Toddler Parenting

Practical Guide to Raising Toddlers and Pre-Schoolers who're grounded, Generous, and Smart in an Over-Entitled World

Barbara S. Johnson

Copyright © 2020 Barbara S. Johnson

All rights reserved. No part of this publication may be reproduced, distributed, or transmitted in any form or by any means, including photocopying, recording, or other electronic or mechanical methods, without the prior written permission of the publisher, except in the case of brief quotations embodied in critical reviews and specific other non-commercial uses permitted by copyright law.

Table of Contents

TODDLER PARENTING 1

INTRODUCTION 4

CHAPTER 1 7
   WHAT TO KNOW ABOUT PARENTING 7

CHAPTER 2 11
   HOW TO ENJOY PARENTING YOUR CHILD 11
      Positive Solutions to Raise a youngster 12
      What to Check Before You Right-Off Children 15

CHAPTER 3 16
   FAIL-PROOF WAYS OF RAISING A KID 16

CHAPTER 4 22
   HOW TO IMPROVE CHILD'S BEHAVIOUR 22
      Prioritize guidelines 23
      Child Rearing Tips 26

CHAPTER 5 29
   THE NINETEEN COMMANDMENTS OF TODDLER SELF-DISCIPLINE 29

CHAPTER 6 35
   COMMON CONCERNS INTENDED FOR PARENTS OF TODDLERS 35
      Helping SMALL KIDS cope with Sibling Competition and Rivalry 36
      Raising YOUR KID without Yelling 37
      Parent Coaching 37

CHAPTER 7 39
   CHILD SELF-DISCIPLINE TECHNIQUES THAT WORKS 39

ACKNOWLEDGEMENTS 48

Introduction

*Are you tired of power struggles, tantrums, and searching for the right **approach,** look no further*. You're about to discover the practical tools you need to transform your parenting in a positive, proven way.

What do you do with a little kid who…won't brush her teeth…screams in his car seat…pinches the baby…refuses to eat vegetables…throws books in the library…runs rampant in the supermarket? Organized by common challenges and conflicts, this book is an essential manual of communication strategies, including a chapter that addresses the special needs of children with sensory processing and autism spectrum disorders.

Based on the latest research on brain development and extensive scientific experience with parents, Barbara S. Johnson's approach is as simple as it is valid with the philosophy that fosters an emotional connection with your children, also to create a real and lasting difference. When you have that vital connection, you don't need to threaten, nag, plead, bribe, or even punish.

This concise book includes fresh insights and suggestions as well as the author's time-tested methods to solve common problems and build foundations for lasting relationships, including innovative ways to:

- Cope with your child's negative feelings, such as frustration, anger, and disappointment.

- Express your strong feelings without being hurtful.

- Engage your child's willing cooperation.

- Set firm limits and maintain goodwill.

- Use alternatives to punishment that promote self-discipline.

- Understand the difference between helpful and unhelpful appraisal.

- Resolve family conflicts peacefully.

Toddlers are constantly changing, and they can quickly become overwhelmed by it all. When faced with the meltdowns that toddlers are known for, it can be challenging to know which toddler discipline techniques will best help your child grow into a stronger, more kind person.

This book is a groundbreaking guide to raising responsible, capable, happy kids. It's the ultimate book on how to effectively communicate and raise your child.

Chapter 1

What to Know About Parenting

Discovering and learning how exactly to flow perfectly using your kids and how to assist these to walk through their transition from infant to toddler, is vital to both parents, guardians, and caregivers.

The progressive pattern from the child's growth could possibly be put into various areas, namely;

· Physical development: This includes the child's physical growth (increase in size).

· Primary movement skills: The control of huge moving toys which frequently let the child to stroll, operate, jump, rise and walk properly.

· Vision: The ability to see closely and translate what's noticed.

· Hearing and speech: The ability to hear, obtain info, and procedure it, be aware (interpretation), aswell as the capability to realise and find out about words and utilize it allowing you to connect effectively.

- Sociable: The capability to hook up towards the world through others.

Although it's better to utilize a graph to define intervals of advancement, it is critical to remember that improvement is continuous.

There could be a variety of what might look like 'abnormal' development. Nevertheless, experts make us recognize that might be milestones that want to be performed by a generation at a specific phase of their lives.

A YEAR AGED

In a year old kids, the normal child can have another abilities:

- Physical and motion skills.

- An average one-year-old toddler's body mass.

- Triple the delivery weight.

- Grow to a height of 50 percent over delivery height.

- Have involve some 1 - 8 teeth.

- Draw to stand.

- Walk with help or alone.

- Sit back without help.

- Bang two blocks with each other.

- Flip through the pages from the book by flicking many pages at the same time.

- Possess a pincer grasp.

- Rest 8-10 hours at night time and look at a handful of naps.

- Sensory and cognitive advancement.

- Understanding how to eat independently.

- Run after an easy-moving object.

- Responds to his/her name.

- Understands a lot of words.

- Can easily say mom, dad, with least other terms.

- Understand basic commands.

- Attempt to replicate pet noises.

- Connect titles with items.

- Understands that products exist, even though they aren't seen.

Chapter 2

How to Enjoy Parenting Your Child

You have survived the sleepless evenings and never-ending feeding cycles of the newborn stage, you experienced a while to cuddle cute baby cheeks and possess a look into every new developing milestone, and before long, that phase of life is finished.

Parenting young kids is related to stepping right into a fresh world; as kids are acquainted in performing things such as for example:

They could speak - however, the standard term they use is obviously "no."

They could walk - however, they could also try to escape from you in parking lots.

They might be impartial - this happens usually every time they are receiving old; within age 2-4.

Here are some tips to ensure that children and pre-schoolers give a method of measuring respect using their parents. Keeping the partnership using your child is important, significant, and healthful aswell as understand how to relish these a long time of training.

Positive Solutions to Raise a youngster

How to favorably parent your child

If you're much like parents, you intend to go directly into discipline, because not going straight into the discipline stage might help the toddler build-up the sense of self-discipline; but when you miss this part, parenting them might be a headache in comparison with a pleasure.

You're probably going to create a never-ending power challenges, intense, weird behavior, and legendary meltdowns.

Positive parenting requires a different approach. This ideology helps us relax and connect good with this children (despite the fact that they might be misbehaving), it'll support them through psychological issues and teach them lessons with techniques that's most dependable.

This sort of parenting really helps to improve the child's behavior, this implies whenever your kid starts acting up, you need to put generation, developing stage, and brain maturity in mind. You might find yourself realizing that your kid is confused with regards to a particular situation to get needed rest.

Every stage made have become relevant solutions and strategies that work; solutions that produce you feel relaxed and in charge.

Okay, Let's discuss how parents can discipline young kids. But first , we will clarify between "self-discipline" and "consequence."

"Punishment/consequence" is targeted on creating a penalty that creates some sort of agony to instruct your kid. "Self-discipline," around the excess hands, seeks to steer your kid, assisting them to secure a far better solution to regulate the problem down the road instead of punishing.

It might appear to be a small assortment of words;

however, it might make an enormous difference in mere how you react to your kid. The pattern of training must not be specialized in insults (or in case you have been raised with parents who used punishment), you might use that just like a yardstick and commence viewing your kid as "bad" or "misbehaving" or "bratty." It may seem that they don't have to "escape utilizing their bad behavior" or by punishing them, they'll learn their lessons.

Regrettably, this won't create a sensible relationship, and you will probably dislike parenting through a child years.

Nevertheless, if you observe your kid, after being punished, you might feel compassionate. You'd have to search for ways to use them, support them because they struggle, or react with sympathy.

It isn't really the "discipline" you're acquainted with; however, it's rather an excellent way to create your child's psychological intelligence, enhance their problem-solving abilities, grow sympathy for others, and maintain your relationship strong and healthy.

What to Check Before You Right-Off Children

Child Meltdowns and Tantrums

Encourage your kid's problem-solving skills using the actions below before you correct or suggest a lot better solution.

No-one can throw a tantrum more advanced than a youngster. It's a full-body encounter that often leaves parents overwhelmed, surprised, and ashamed.

Thankfully, tantrums are typical through the toddler and preschooler years. It's hard to grasp everything about the toddler simultaneously.

Using ethical child-rearing principle, you can decrease the level of tantrums and the potency of the meltdowns your kid encounters during the day.

Chapter 3

Fail-proof Ways of Raising a kid

With this chapter, we've highlighted various methodologies for raising your kid, which if we consider, would help to make a massive difference inside your parenting journey.

Leading by example:

It truly is natural to need to change something when it seems uncontrollable. Nevertheless, we really can't control several other things. If we make an effort to control a youngster, this usually leads to contention in power. We're able to control our personal behavior and try once you can to permit child imitate us. Partnering using your child and working together as a team most time provides positive effect through connection and co-operation. Conversely, control creates a routine amount of resistance.

Concentrate on the positivity:

Did you ever hear that "Whatever you concentrate on develops?" This perspective offers a substantial influence around the thoughts, emotions, and feelings. Practice this by informing your kid just what they might be successful at, also, remove time and energy to celebrate what's working well to them. Getting devoted to these advantages reinforce a child and leaves everyone's senses more strengthened.

Connection is key:

Small children could possibly be indie immediately, yet they'll remain exceptionally emotionally reliant on us. This is why relationship plays a significant role in toddlerhood. Connecting using your kid amidst a hardcore position helps them gain psychological balance. When there are a sound connection, just a little child will learn, develop, and flourish.

Focus on be studied notice of:

It's normal for humans to notice and appearance noticed. The very fact that parents are already old and possess vast knowledge of life doesn't imply we should appear down upon a toddler's emotions, feelings, and thoughts. The quickest way to make a child to avoid hearing you is to avoid hearing them.

Practically all emotions and feelings are alright, however, not absolutely all actions:

As humans, we are programmed to go to a full spectral range of emotions. Allowing your kid notice that emotions and feelings are okay to help change their mindset, but validating emotions won't mean you need to condone some of their outstanding behaviours. Rather than shutting down their emotions and feelings, support your kid to sort them out. You may help them workout how exactly to communicate their feelings and emotions with proper behavior.

Get considering their behavior:

Attention is probably the very most dependable tools we've in child-rearing. Getting and considering your toddler's behavior enables you to find out about them within the deeper level, and prevents you from becoming the assets and court. This attention creates a connection, time and energy to respond rather than reacting if you are feeling disappointed.

Focus on what's fueling the behavior, not the action itself:

Your toddler's behavior is powered by emotions, feelings, and needs. This is why the simplest way to improve behavior isn't merely by concentrating on the action itself. It truly is by focusing on the principal act, which might be the actual cause. Dealing with their emotions, feelings, and needs changes behavior.

Performance could be the main work:

The principal job a toddler offers is to produce periods. Producing out period for unstructured creativity that's enjoyed provides your kid with a wholesome sense of autonomy and control because they get out and grasp new abilities.

Help them encounter expectations:

Small kids possess spent slightly while on earth but nonetheless need more time to comprehend so lots of things about how precisely to learn this globe. Sometimes they could be developmentally struggling, and they are likely to inform you about utilizing their behavior.

The simplest way you may help them isn't by insults and abuse, but by teaching them the talents, they have to understand and meet up with the expectation down the road.

We request you to take a breath and invite it to test gradually. Award yourself a massive appraisal, awaken every day, and do the very best you can.

Change doesn't happen overnight -- it needs a while, practice, and support. Every day serves as an opportunity and a foundation to be ready for what will happen next.

If you create any mistake, never let it put you down. Most parents also make mistakes. Just use that probability to learn. Every single minute is surely an invitation to begin once again.

Chapter 4

How to Improve Child's Behaviour

Small kids are subconsciously known with regards to childish display and extra behavioral issues, therefore following proper parenting ideas is key to encourage eager observation, listening, and rendering assistance when needed.

Getting acquainted with children can make life frustrating. As much once we intend to exist fair enough, children cannot move as quickly even as we like these to; because they will usually have to communicate their need, without the limit (they end up having bargaining and dissatisfaction). This usually can result in tantrums and misbehaviors.

Nevertheless, you may train your kid to act sound giving superior guidelines plus some regular with love.

- Useful Suggestions to Improve Child's Behaviour

- Carefully examine these valuable tips.

- Display your feelings

Ensure that so on you display to your kid outnumbers any punishment. Hugs, kisses, and good-nature reassure your kid of how much you value them; the same manner, compliments, and attention could also motivate your kid.

Prioritize guidelines

Instead of overloading your kid with rules and principles from your perspective that gets him/her furious, prioritize the ones aimed toward health and safety first, and continuously put tips in the future. Help your kid adhere to the guidelines by just childproofing your house and removing some lure.

Prevent Tantrums

It's regular for a youngster to obtain temper tantrums also to reduce the pace of recurrence. To time or know the potency of your kid's tantrums, you should;

Understand your kid's limitations: Your kid may misbehave if he/she won't understand precisely what you are requesting.

See how to check on and adjust your rules and principles; Rather than saying, "Stop striking," you can offer recommendations and actions to accomplish one more thing instead.

Consider 'NO' as an indicator of progress: Don't overreact whenever your kid says no, alternatively you can make an effort, compelling them to perform it again. You may try to produce the work fun by playing any game. Your kid could possibly be more likely to perform what you would like if you make the work fun.

Pick your fights: If you state 'NO' to everything, your kid will most likely obtain discouraged. Carefully observe occasions if it's okay to convey YES.

Offer options, when feasible: Encourage your kid's independence by, for instance, simply allowing him/her to select several pajamas or a bedtime tale.

Prevent situations that may trigger disappointment or tantrums: For instance, prevent giving your kid fun toys that are too advanced on her behalf or him. Avoid extended outings where your kid must relax actually if he/she can or cannot perform. Also recognize that kids will require action out when they're exhausted, hungry, ill, or within an unfamiliar environment.

Follow the program: Maintain a day to day routine, meaning your kid will know very well what to expect.

Motivate communication: Help remind your kid to use terms expressing his/her emotions. In case your kid isn't very outspoken, consider teaching them baby sign vocabulary to avoid disappointment. (Checkout Baby Sign Language Simplified <http://getbook.at/bslsp> by Regina Williams).

Set an example: Children understand how to do this just by viewing what their parents also do. The simplest way of showing your kid how to act will be to create an example on her behalf or him to look at.

Enforce effects: Despite your better efforts, eventually, your kid may break the guidelines. Ignore small signs of anger, for instance; "if a youngster strike, kicks or screams for an extended period"; cautiously support a child with whatever problem it truly is. Consider using another child-raising suggestions to motivate your kid to cooperate.

Child Rearing Tips

- Organic Consequences

Allow your kid to start to see the consequence of his/her actions, as long as they're risk-free. For instance, in case your kid throws and breaks a toy, he/she won't support the gadget again, to avoid repetition of damage.

- Reasonable Consequences

Be sure everything your kid needs for his/her activities is well provided, and make him/her recognize that if he/she won't grab the play toys carefully, you need to place the enjoying of toys aside for all those other day. Support your kid with the countless actions, if needed. In case your kid won't cooperate, make him/her know the consequence.

- Withholding Liberties

In case your kid misbehaves, ensure that you avoid within his/her reach that a very important factor making him/her become that, e.g., a favorite toy or something associated with his/her misbehavior.

- Timeout

Whenever your kid acts up, decrease to his/her level, briefly and calmly clarify why the behavior is undesirable. If the indigent behavior proceeds, guide your kid to a specified timeout place, preferably a quiet area without interruptions. Enforce the timeout till your kid is relaxed and may concentrate on you. Afterward, assure your kid of so on and demonstrate own for him/her.

- Whatever consequences you select, be constant

Ensure that every single adult who also cares about your kid observes this same guidelines and discipline recommendations.

Also, look out for criticizing your kid's behavior. Spanking, slapping, and shouting at a young child shouldn't become adopted.

Chapter 5

The Nineteen Commandments of Toddler Self-discipline

It isn't great to let your kid get too convenient with rules and implications due to the bond and functional relationship between you and them.

Children that are not necessarily given birth to with sociable abilities frequently have the average indivdual character of survival-of-the-fittest mindset. This is why you should train your kid how to do some things and do them appropriately and securely.

The seed products of self-discipline will bloom later, and you will be very impressed by the fruits from the labour. Listed below are the commandments you need to purchase:

ü Anticipate tight conditions - Certain circumstances and occasions of your mood tend to produce bad behaviour.

There's a simple belief a transition in a single activity to another gives your kid a heads-up, so he's a lot more ready for upgrades.

ü Choose your fights - If you say "No" twenty times every day, the word "no" will eventually lose its value. Prioritize actions into massive, medium, and the ones too minor to make use of.

ü Make using a prevent protection - Create your home child-friendly, and still have affordable expectations. If you obviously move your movie collections from your desk, your kid won't exist enticed to fling everything. If you are taking all your family out to supper, proceed early, and this means you're refusing to have to hold them back.

ü Help to create your claims short and pleasant - Speak the bottom line is phrases, such as "No biting." That is a lot more effective than "Chase; you understand it does not sound more likely to your dog.

ü Distract and refocus - for instance, in case your kid unrolls the entire toilet-paper, efficiently remove her from your own toilet and close the entrance door.

ü   Introduce effects - Your kid must learn the organic results of their behavior. For instance, in the event where he/she fully insists on selecting what pajamas to wear (which requires a long time), after a long time of selection, there is absolutely no time to understand before going to bed - cause: Continuous choosing of pajamas, Effect: Minimal time to learn and discover. The next time, he'd select his pajamas quickly or let you select them for him.

ü   Do not cool-down in order to avoid discord - If you decide that your kid won't take the cereal that she noticed on TV, follow your decision. Later, you will be content you did.

ü   Anticipate offers for interest - Yes, your little angel will work up whenever your attention is generally diverted, building supper or speaking on calling. This is why it's necessary to provide several entertainments (a gadget or an instantaneous treat).

ü   Concentrate round the behavior, not really a child - it's best you say a particular action is terrible, however in no chance in case you inform your kid that he/she is bad.

ü   Give your kid choices - This might make her feel like she's a say. Be sure to prevent offering him/her so many choices.

ü   I've got a tender yell - It is possible to yell, but change your modulation of voice. It usually quantities to nothing when you scream close to the top of the voice; however, the firmness from the voice passes the knowledge across. Remember that you never really had a have to yell.

ü   Catch your kid being good - If you praise your kid if they behave good, he'll do something more often and he may be less inclined to act terribly to get the attention needed. Positive encouragement is generally fertilizer for the super-ego.

ü   Consider action instantly - don't await your kid to usually understand some things, don't think your kid can self-discipline him/herself always.

ü   Closing up being considered a fantastic role model

- If you are quiet under ruthless, your kid will demand the cue. And if you are hot-tempered, if you are irritated, expect that he'll do the same. He's watching you, always watching.

ü	Do treat your kid as if she happens to be a grown-up - A child doesn't need to listen to your extended speech because he/she might not even understand it. For instance, the next time he/she would like to prepare spaghetti improperly, don't cave in way too many lectures, constantly evict her from your kitchen for the night time.

ü	Make using time-outs - once a while, you'd have to consider restricting your kid from playing and do not focus on him first minute for every year old. Starving him through the attention could be the easiest way to get your message through.

Realistically, children under two won't sit down in a corner or inside the seat, and it's really wonderful to allow them to be to the floor kicking and screaming. Simply be sure the time-out location is a secure one.

ü	Change your strategies after some time - What

worked superbly well whenever your son or daughter was 15 weeks probably isn't more likely to work when he's two.

ü   Don't spank - Even if you end up being tempted sometimes, but don't. You will notice a lot more effective approach to acquiring the message across. In case your kid begins striking or kicking you, for example, just display him that it is alright to work with pressure. Finally, if your kid is normally pressing your links for the umpteenth period, and that means you consider you will drop this, make an effort to have a very step backwards. You'll receive a lot better notion which manipulative manners your kid is generally using, and you will get yourself a fresh perspective about how precisely to improve your approach.

Remind your kid that you would like her - That's definitely good to remove a self-discipline conversation with an excellent comment. This shows your kid that you have been ready to proceed instead of adhere to the problem. Also, it reinforces the reason why you set limitation because you prefer her.

Chapter 6

Common concerns intended for Parents of Toddlers

Are you sick and tired of what your kid manages, so you don't possess much strength to transport them back?

Using these assured pointers might help you own a lovely encounter in parenting.

The duty parent face with regards to a child's growth isn't only self-discipline; additionally, there is several other challenges that pop-up subconsciously. Thankfully, almost all problems aren't unique. Few appear to be a satisfactory thing every child must do because they grow older.

Utilizing this can help your reaction when these issues arrive, likewise own it behind your brain that each child differs. You might be an expert using your child, but anytime you observe something unusual or of concern, don't hesitate to talk to the physician or a Mental wellness provider.

Helping SMALL KIDS cope with Sibling Competition and Rivalry

- Parenting a toddler is severe enough, yet devote several additional children in the blend, and suddenly, you have several new challenges accessible.

- Instead of expecting your son or daughter to modify these interpersonal skills easily, supply them with the support they want as they workout how exactly to share toys, make changes, and argue without harming another kid.

The following advice and approaches for parenting children are excellent theoretically; however, they could promptly appear impossible the simple truth is, if you don't understand how to control your anger.

Raising YOUR KID without Yelling

You do not want to yell; however, you intend to put up your better act so you won't injure the children, but there are numerous factors that may necessitate parents shouting - feeling uncontrollable, being unsure of how to react, fretting about how many other people consider you, panicking that you're ruining your child···etc.

Instead of remaining trapped, you may attempt once you can to get your mind from your yelling. Look the tips I've explained, get among the new strategies, which will help give you massive amount persistence, and enable you to remain optimistic.

When you start yelling at your children, maybe it's quite tricky in order to avoid or to shift from unaggressive parent to a confident parent.

You will find occasions your kid will expect you to intensify, nonetheless it shouldn't be every time.

Parent Coaching

Raising small kids and pre-schoolers could possibly be considered a problem, nonetheless it may also be isolating and complicated. An instantaneous Google search can provide you a million different answers, as well as your friends' raising a youngster concept, might not exactly match how you need to parent.

You don't wish to accomplish the entire parenting by yourself; there is also support obtainable. Obtaining knowledge on how to Parent a youngster in books is generally safe (above 70%), sound and non-judgmental as you find training pattern, fantastic for you personally as well as your kid.

If everything previously stated seem overwhelming and that means you don't have any thought on how to start, do not panic. Almost always there is a way, only once we're able to give everything it requires.

Chapter 7

Child Self-discipline Techniques that Works

If you are discouraged using your children anticipations, worry less, disciplining young kids may be difficult.

Denise Marshall, an early-child years educator, once said: "What's 'bad' behavior anyway? Every time a child's description aswell as the parent's instruction tend to be completely different: You inform your kid to place a gadget away. They don't. You see since defiance. They don't need to avoid playing."

Experts agree that children will certainly "misbehave" when our anticipation will be a lot more than their abilities. For instance, it isn't convenient to anticipate a youngster to check out a string of instructions, or even to remember a guideline after being told only one time.

A Daycare expert clarifies, "You will need to keep words simple. A lot is occurring of their minds. It's essential to repeat yourself; otherwise it'll get overlooked."

To keep objectives realistic, it truly is beneficial to find out about developmental elements that impacts toddler behavior:

- Social abilities

At age 1.5 years, toddlers are beginning to consider getting and various children. Nevertheless the guidelines of sociable play aren't instinctive, kids have to be trained regarding taking converts and getting mild. Actually, intense behaviour like biting is generally normal. "It's developmental. It is the way they respond."

- Self-control

Most of the defiance that men and women attribute to toddler behavior is due to their particular limited capacity to modify their impulses. Your girlfriend might recognize that chucking food from your own high seat is a no-no, yet try because she feels the desire to see her mac and cheese move splat onto the bottom could possibly be overpowering.

Alternatively, whenever a toddler's urges and wishes are discouraged, the reaction may be intense.

- Psychological regulation

Kids have trouble understanding their feelings, aside from controlling them. They need support, identify and deal utilizing their emotions. Making use of your reassuring hugs, maybe it's good for expose self-soothing techniques.

- Sympathy

Small children are simply just learning other folks, the reason why they may be self-centered. Because they have trouble with empathy- they don't really observe that others respond adversely to discomfort or disappointment. This also explains regarding the reasons a youngster may react inappropriately to some other child's feelings, like laughing whenever a playmate pinches another to have the toy.

- Comprehension

How can a young child abide by instructions when he/she

doesn't even know the results of not adhering? Since vocabulary and attention abilities are simply just growing in toddlerhood, it is critical to never overestimate what kids may comprehend. "Children could know very well what parents are requesting, nevertheless the parents need to encourage them."

Even in case your kid know very well what you're stating, he cannot be offering you attention. "I must say i have no idea any child who listens frequently. You need to obtain because of their level.

- What works

How exactly can someone really guide your child's conduct? The same as your kid is wanting out her behavior, you will need to try your self-discipline strategies, predicated on her age, character as well as your beliefs. Listed below are the very best strategies:

1. Prevent

"Constantly think forward: 'How can you really

understand this to effective every day,.' You can find this effect by establishing a fantastic encircling to great behavior. In case your kid is actually into dressing herself, be sure to possess a whole lot of trousers with flexible waists and shirts that are easy to put on to lessen aggravation or a young child who's starving, thirsty, exhausted or hurried will be a lot more likely to misbehave.

2. Offer choices

Because young kids try out self-reliance, it's important to supply them secure, reasonable probabilities to convey things such as for example: "Would you like your juice in the deep glass or the green cup?" "Would you like to go directly to the carpark in your automobile or the newborn stroller?"

3. Supervise

This might not look like a self-discipline tool; nevertheless, you can't support your kid discover out appropriate actions if you are not there to teach him. This doesn't mean stepping directly into every single problem but instead guiding them about how precisely to start out it.

4. Organized targets and consequences

Kids can't follow the rules if indeed they can not even understand the gravity of the guidelines. Ensure that you produce the instructions and guidelines simple; "Establish eye-to-eye contact and be sure she's nodding when you talk to her."

5. Display and tell

Young kids are apparent, they virtualize every single thing happening around them; consequently, you'd have to model the behavior you want. So whatever change you want these to see, you'd wish to accomplish it first.

6. Compliment

As single-minded as young kids are, they nonetheless need compliments. Make sure to compliment your boy when he put his food shared; this usually helps your relationship. "Children need a great deal of attention; that's our parents.

7. Refocus

If any situation arises that may warrant any weird behavior, distract them with something they choose to accomplish In the case whereby your 2½-year-old is disappointed that her old sibling won't discuss her new doll, state, "Let's get the peel of stickers at your kitchen desk." And for this generation, children choose to help.

Redirection may possibly also "unstick" your kid from a No-No. If she's attracted to be a magnet to Grandma's audio system, get her connected with any fresh activity.

8. Remove

Parents should create an effective, silent place wherever your kid could possibly be with you. When he offers dropped control, carefully remove him from where he's. It is not an outcome, but instead a location to relax. The sofa, a step in the stairs or a spot round the carpet such as cushy cushions, isn't a horrible idea.

9. Consider what you do

Though it seems sensible to talk to a young child after an incident of misbehavior, that's pointless with toddlers.

10. State sorry

You can create a young child feel bad, if you apologize after.

11. "No, no, almost no, no⋯."

It's more best for display kids what direction to visit instead of never knowing what next to perform. Rather than "shouting NO," try once you can to hire a peaceful modulation of voice" and state it silently.

12. Establish obvious goals

Ensure that your guidelines are apparent and he/she actually can hear you: " If you splash normal water through the tub once again, I'll consider those glass aside."

Old toddlers might react if you describe why: "Splashing normal water to the floor is generally dangerous. It could make the majority of us fall."

13. Provide options

"Would you like to put water inside your flask or your cup?". Providing them with choices means we are carrying them along, and they also could get confusing in activity.

14. Remove

If splashing normal water continues, remove her in the tub and clarify why: "You're stubborn; therefore, you're much more likely to need to turn out."

15. Consequences

Ask her to utilize tidy in the splashed normal water - showing the results of her activities: "Water must exist cleaned up because of the fact someone can slide and get hurt."

Acknowledgements

The Glory of this book success goes to God Almighty and my beautiful Family, Fans, Readers & well-wishers, Customers, and Friends for their endless support and encouragement.

www.ingramcontent.com/pod-product-compliance
Lightning Source LLC
Chambersburg PA
CBHW081159070526
44583CB00021B/2908